NEW YORK
VINTAGE POSTER

COLORING BOOK FOR ADULTS

PUBLISHED BY

HARPER & BROTHERS NEW YORK

★ Mrs. HENRY DRAPER

HARPER'S CHRISTMAS

★ Mrs. HENRY DRAPER

PEOPLE
WE
PASS

Stories of Life
among the Masses
of New York City

By

Julian Ralph

Illustrated

Harper & Brothers
Publishers

Collier's

OCTOBER 3D 1903

HARVESTING WHEAT IN THE WEST

VOLUME XXXII : NUMBER 1 : PRICE 10 CENTS

CADET DAYS.

A STORY OF
WEST-POINT
BY
CAPT. CHARLES KING U.S.A.

ILLUSTRATED

HARPER & BROTHERS
NEW-YORK

VOLUME XXVII NO 19   AUGUST 10 1901   PRICE TEN CENTS

COLLIER'S
ILLUSTRATED WEEKLY

"TRYING OUT" THE AMERICA'S CUP DEFENDERS OFF NEWPORT

Edward Penfield

POSTER
CALENDAR
1897

Published by
R.H. Russell & Son
NEW YORK

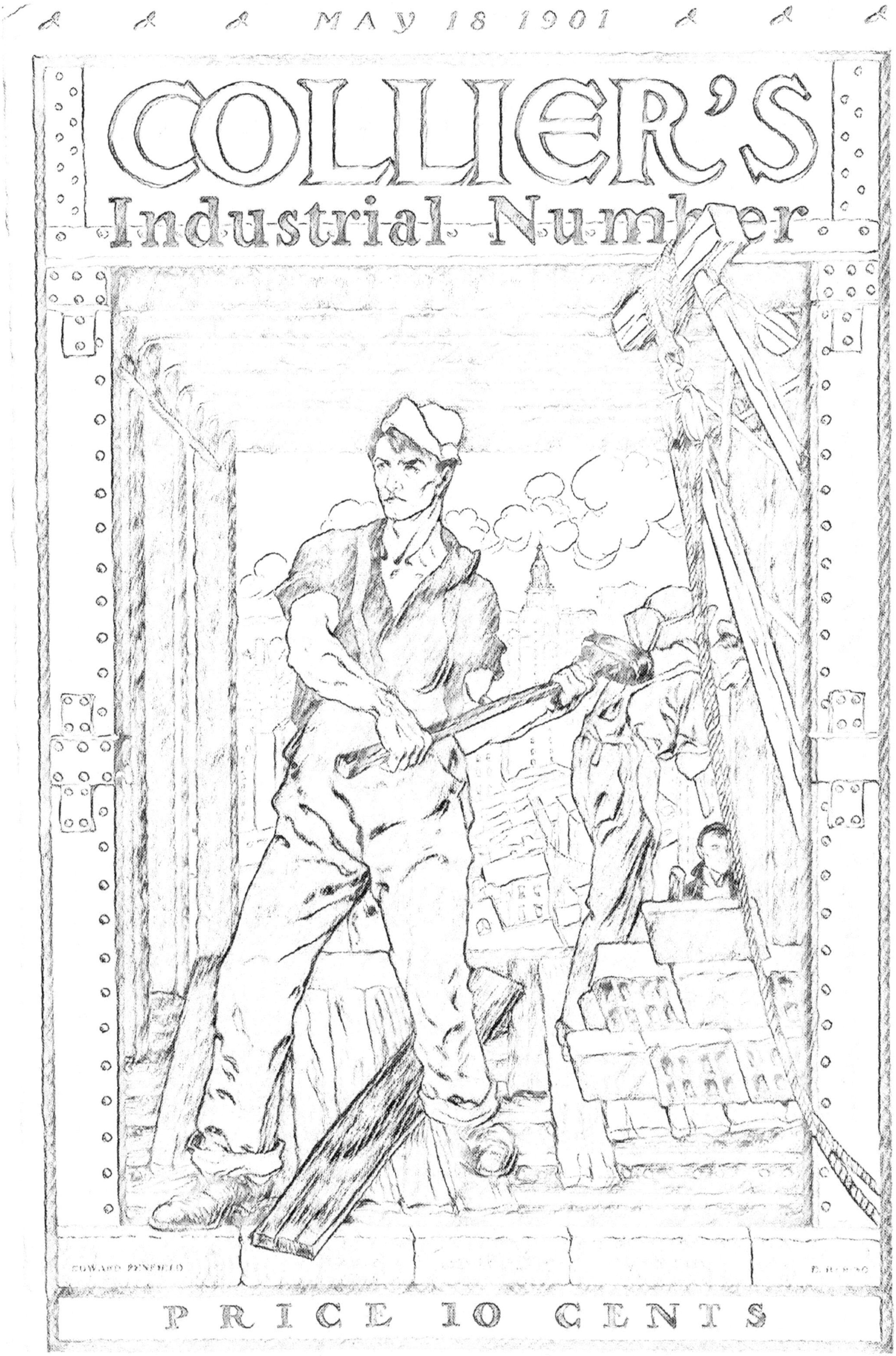
MAY 18 1901
COLLIER'S
Industrial Number
PRICE 10 CENTS

MAY 25 1901 PRICE TEN CENTS

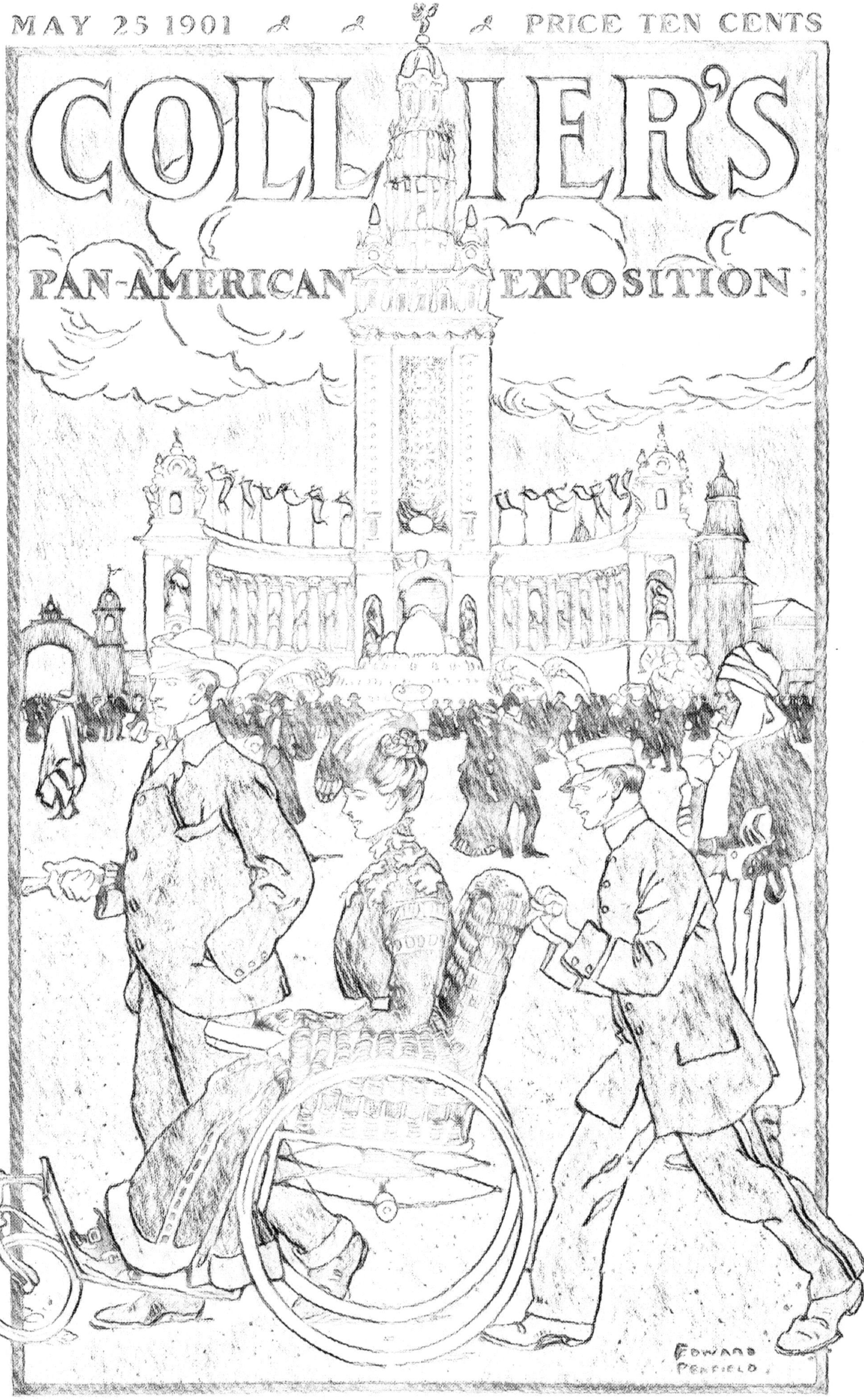

HARPER'S

JANUARY CONTAINS

COLLIER'S

Greater New-York

Petrus Stuyvesant Governor of New Amsterdam

JANUARY 25
1902

1647

PRICE
TEN CENTS

THE SUMMER-PORCH NUMBER OF
THE LADIES' HOME JOURNAL

AUGUST 1908   THE CURTIS PUBLISHING COMPANY PHILADELPHIA   FIFTEEN CENTS

STIRRING TIMES IN AUSTRIA DESCRIBED BY MARK TWAIN

IN HARPER'S MARCH

LIPPINCOTT'S

JUNE

INTERNATIONAL ATHLETICS

OCTOBER

25 CENTS

OUTING

AN ILLVSTRATED MAGAZINE
OF SPORT TRAVEL ADVENTVRE
AND COVNTRY LIFE

EDITED BY CASPAR WHITNEY

NEW YORK & LONDON

COUNTRY LIFE

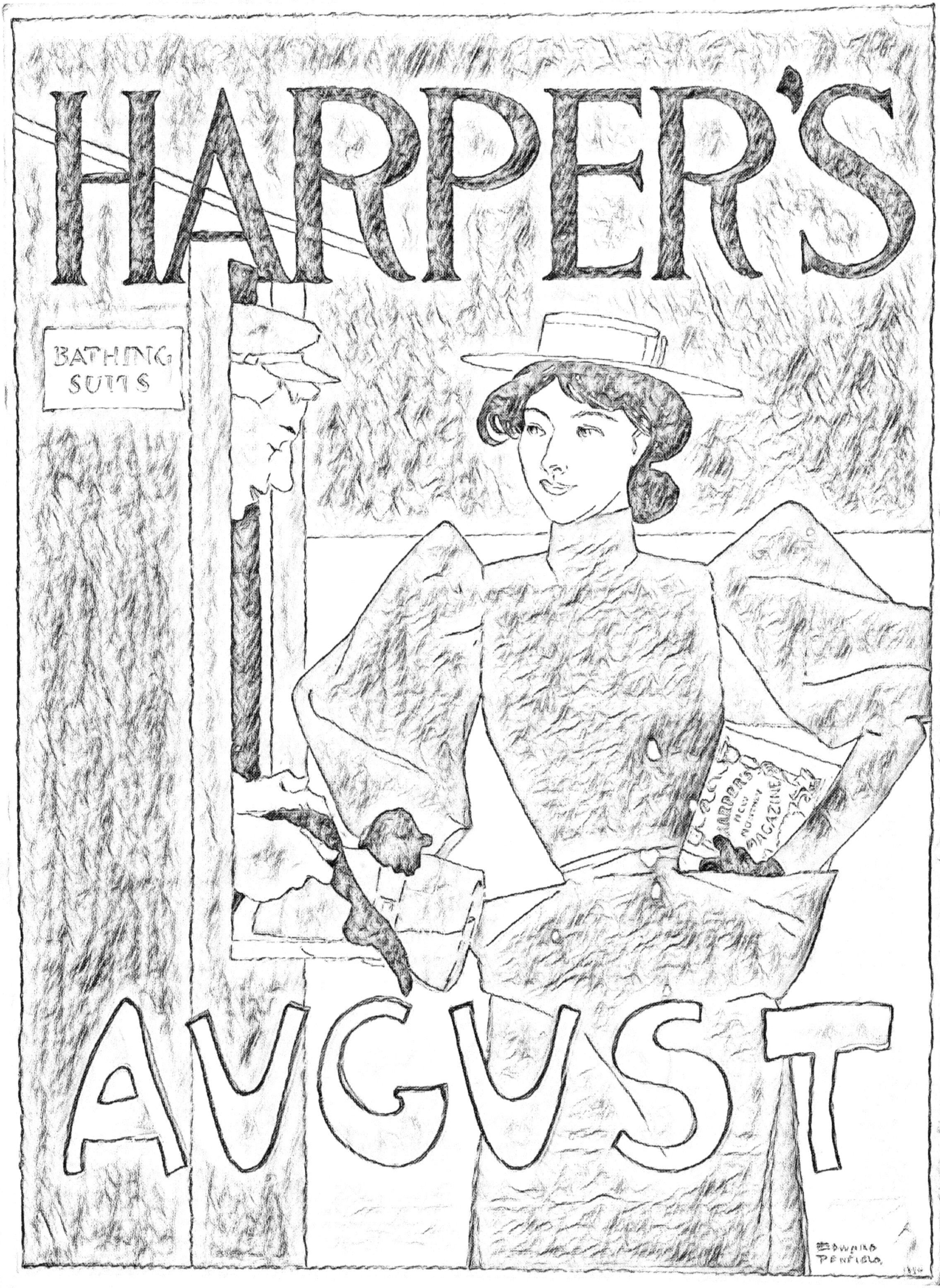
HARPER'S
BATHING SUITS
AUGUST

VOLUME XXVII NO 18   AUGUST 3 1901   PRICE TEN CENTS

COLLIER'S
ILLUSTRATED WEEKLY

The Great Strike
By CARROLL D. WRIGHT
United States Commissioner of Labor

Join Us >> bit.ly/get_sample_free

- Get Free "Reviw Copies" of our New releases
- Exclusive offers and book giveaways
- More events from our community

Thank you

www.ingramcontent.com/pod-product-compliance
Lightning Source LLC
Chambersburg PA
CBHW081601280526
45788CB00011B/3535